An Oasis in Time
Seven Thoughts for the Seventh Day

MAGGID

Rabbi Benji Levy

An Oasis in
TIME
Seven Thoughts for the Seventh Day

Maggid Books

An Oasis in Time
Seven Thoughts for the Seventh Day

First Edition, 2019

Maggid Books
An imprint of Koren Publishers Jerusalem Ltd.

POB 8531, New Milford, CT 06776-8531, USA
& POB 4044, Jerusalem 9104001, Israel
www.maggidbooks.com

ISBN 978-1-59264-531-2, *paperback*

A CIP catalogue record for this title is
available from the British Library

Printed and bound in Israel

She opens her mouth with wisdom,
and the law of kindness is on her tongue.

Proverbs 31:26

In memory of

Brenda Jankelowitz z"l

and

Rose Fekete z"l

Friends, colleagues, role models,
tour guides for life, and lovers of Shabbat

୫ର

Contents

The Creation of Rest –
a Rest from Creation

The book of Genesis, as its name suggests, describes the great-est creative act in the history of the universe. It commences with the very conception of creation itself, the foundation from which all matter was formed, launching the world into a perpetual state of development.

Newton's first law of inertia states that objects will not move unless acted upon. God's creation was this seminal cre-ative act, the beginning of all beginnings, setting the wheels of our ever-expanding universe in motion and spinning the world around its own axis. And yet this same law of inertia states that objects will not stop moving unless acted upon by an external force, such that in a vacuum these metaphorical wheels would spin *ad infinitum* unless stopped by an external impetus. The biblical account of Creation highlights the same Creator who creates the universe on the first day as He who creates Shabbat, the day of rest, on the seventh. Ordinarily, rest is seen as the cessation of work. In the context of Creation, however, the Shabbat day of rest represents the ultimate form of creativity. God's act of rest is, in essence, as revolutionary as

His act of creation. When everything else is whole and complete, rest is the only ingredient lacking. Therefore, "when the seventh day came, rest came, and the universe was complete."[1] On the seventh day, God created rest, and, through this rest, He completed Creation.

Since God handed the Garden of Eden to humanity "to work and to preserve it,"[2] we have been in a constant process of building and developing everything around us. The birth of the marketplace, the industrial revolution, and the invention of the Internet are but a few of the many breakthroughs that have shifted paradigms and given rise to new worlds that are evolving at an exponential rate. On the first day, God said: "Let there be light."[3] And indeed, the energy from this first primordial light continues to pulse daily through humanity's innovation as a partner in the ongoing process of Creation. Yet our balance has been skewed towards one extreme. Our preoccupation with "working" through building and developing has resulted in a failure to successfully "preserve." Shabbat helps us focus on the importance of balancing between preservation and work.

FROM REST TO RESTORATION

Today, rest is often synonymous with switching off our minds and switching on external stimuli in their stead. People flick through channels on TV, flip through pages of a magazine, or surf sites on the Internet, allowing a break from the frenetic pace of modern life. This rest can be passive. Initially

---

1. Genesis Rabba 10:9.
2. Genesis 2:15.
3. Genesis 1:3.

it feels good, but if prolonged, it can lead to a greater feeling of lethargy.

Shabbat is different. The rest we pursue on Shabbat has more of an active nature. It requires the channeling of a different kind of energy. If enacted correctly, this active rest leads to a feeling of rejuvenation. Passive rest is incidental; active rest is intentional. Rather than sitting back and relaxing while life passes us by, active rest is about engaging in life and savoring the moments and relationships that truly give us meaning.

Celebrating Shabbat, in its truest sense, is the ultimate tutorial in active rest; it is the journey from rest to restoration. There are a plethora of pathways that Shabbat places before us, relating to every sphere of our lives. The pages that follow provide seven thoughts for this awesome seventh day, offering seven unique entry points to the oasis in time that is Shabbat.

Throughout the years, I have shared many ideas contained in this book with my thousands of students and teachers, friends, and colleagues where I have most recently learned and taught, through Moriah College and Mosaic United, Mizrachi and Kadima, and I look forward to feedback as we further develop these concepts together. I would like to make particular mention of Abi Blackman and JJ Kimche, who were my thought partners and editorial sounding board in producing this work, and the tremendous team at Maggid Books who brought it to life: Rabbi Reuven Ziegler, Sarah Levin, Rachel Kellner, and Shira Finson, under the stellar leadership of my dear friends Matthew and Yehoshua Miller.

As I share thoughts that started with and continue through my family, I cannot help but mention my gratitude to them. Thank you to my dear parents, Debbie and Geoff, and siblings, Jon Jon, Lior, Rachel, Brad, Gabi, and Eitan, who made Shabbat so special for me as I grew up, turning this theory into practice. And of course, I am eternally grateful to my soulmate, Renana, who infuses everything we do with the uniqueness of Shabbat, and our incredible children, Shayna, Yehuda, Lital, and Amalia, who imbue my Shabbat with more meaning than I ever knew possible. Finally, it may seem strange, but I would like to thank Shabbat – my private sanctuary which cuts through the noise, anchors my soul, and recalibrates my trajectory, serving as the true "source of my blessing."

With this lived experience in mind, in the following pages I will explore the great themes of Shabbat, whose wisdom is millennia old and yet absolutely relevant to some of contemporary society's most pressing issues.

The first two chapters discuss the personal and individual aspects of Shabbat, exploring how Shabbat yields important perspectives on our relationship with our own selves, our minds, and our spiritual yearnings. I then discuss how Shabbat characterizes the Jewish attitude to humanity and humankind, how it informs the universalist side of our religious worldview and enjoins us to pursue an authentic, inclusive form of social justice. Finally, I explore how Shabbat is at the heart of two ideas that constitute Judaism's most important intellectual contributions to human civilization: monotheism and messianism.

Through undertaking this journey from ideas to ideals, I hope that we will gain a deeper appreciation of Judaism's ancient and beloved weekly reboot and the underlying structures of our spiritual and intellectual world, thereby illuminating a greater appreciation for our place and purpose within it.

One

Shabbat and the Self

Being Human: Human Being

We like to believe that we are free. In reality, this sense of freedom is often an illusion:

> Man's sin is in his failure to live what he is.
> Being the master of the earth,
> Man forgets that he is the servant of God.[1]

Indeed, we can choose what we want to be, how we want to feel; we can choose where we want to go and with whom we want to live. We all have rights, and we don't hesitate to use them in order to exert our "freedom." Yet it is often all too easy for us to forget that with rights come responsibilities. It is precisely because we live free and democratic lives that we have an obligation, a duty, to use our rights and freedoms to improve the society we live in.

---

1. Abraham Joshua Heschel, *I Asked for Wonder: A Spiritual Anthology* (New York, 1986), 43.

The question of freedom opens up a new conversation that engages young and old alike. Is freedom the mere ability to do whatever we want, whenever we want? Is freedom simply the right to self-determination, to live autonomously as an individual? Does being free absolve us of our responsibilities and obligations to the Other?

We often hear people blaming religion for restricting independence. After all, how can a religious person be truly free if they have to live within such a defined framework? This very question of self-rule within a world of rules and laws beyond the self can also be applied to Shabbat. Seemingly mired in a long list of constraints,[2] how can Shabbat be a conduit for self-discovery and soulful emancipation?

POSITIVE AND NEGATIVE LIBERTY

One approach to addressing this question is to appreciate the extent to which the definitions of freedom and liberty have become so distorted over the last century that we have practically forgotten their essence. Freedom is not something that is simply granted to us; rather, it is something that we ourselves create and destroy. Sometimes we lose our free will through the way we use our free will. There is no such thing as absolute freedom, and none of us are entirely free. We are all defined and influenced in some way by our upbringings, our socio-economic status, our genes, and a variety of other factors and circumstances. Today, more than ever before, we are enslaved by a wide array of constructs, including society, fashion, image, technology, social media,

---

2. There are 39 primary categories of constraints, known as *melakhot*, in Jewish law. See Mishna Shabbat 7:2.

and work. Isaiah Berlin, the well-known Jewish social and political philosopher, speaks of two types of freedom, negative and positive.[3] Negative liberty is the absence of obstacles or constrictions. Positive liberty is the autonomy to act in such a way as to take control of one's life and realize one's fundamental purpose.

On Shabbat, negative liberty is used to create space for positive liberty to flourish, through limitations that enhance our freedom in a positive sense. The famous musician Stevie Wonder was known to embody this attitude. Incredibly, he saw his blindness as a gift. Perhaps we can only truly appreciate the essence of Shabbat through the vision of a blind musician. We can all recall a time in our childhood that we volunteered to be blindfolded for a fun activity. In that temporary period of disorientation, we were forced to rely on our other senses. Stevie Wonder was able realize that, in the process of having to endure a lifetime of blindness, his limitation would free him from the distractions of everyday sights and enhance his freedom to develop his other senses.[4] It is this attitude that allowed him to become one of the greatest musicians of our time. While Shabbat limits some senses, it enhances others. In this way, negative liberty is used to remove everyday obstacles and allow true positive liberty to emerge.

Thousands of years ago when the people of Israel left Egypt, they were given freedom. But this was a freedom *from* slavery; it was not yet a directed freedom *to* achieve a purpose.

---

3. Isaiah Berlin, "Two Concepts of Liberty," in *Four Essays on Liberty* (Oxford, 1969).
4. Mary Bates, "Superpowers for the Blind and Deaf," *Scientific American*, September 18, 2012.

To learn how to become truly free, in the positive sense, we must decide what we have been given freedom to do. The Eisenhower Matrix teaches us the importance of breaking free from the urgent to be able to focus on the important.[5] It took the Israelites forty years to understand this life lesson. It is a lesson that is consistently realized through Shabbat. And it is a lesson that we are still learning today.

Shabbat is discussed a number of times in the Torah. In fact, the Torah describes a distinct association between Shabbat and the Exodus from Egypt:

> And you shall remember that you were a servant in the land of Egypt, and the Lord your God brought you out with a mighty Hand and an outstretched Arm; therefore, the Lord your God commanded you to keep the Sabbath day... [6]

What, though, is the connection between our time as slaves in Egypt and keeping Shabbat?

Through experiencing Shabbat, we are able to achieve ultimate freedom. An inextricable element of our obligation to keep Shabbat is that we must first work for six days. Thus, for six days, transient matters may occupy the majority of our day. The seventh day, however, is one of emancipation, where we are reminded each week anew of what liberty actually means. To truly be a free person, we must first exercise that freedom

---

5. The Eisenhower Matrix divides tasks into four quadrants based on whether or not they are categorized as important and/or urgent. See James Clear, "Use the 'Eisenhower Box' to Stop Wasting Time and Be More Productive," *Entrepreneur*, April 29, 2014.

6. Deuteronomy 5:14.

effectively – to create and build, to initiate and invent – for part of living as dignified, free beings is the ability to develop the world and utilize its resources responsibly. But equally, we are duty-bound to recognize the limits of our creativity: to understand that our freedom to create and cultivate nature must also be balanced with constraint. By restraining ourselves from physical creativity for one day each week, we create the freedom to recognize that there is a greater purpose beyond our own success. Through self-restraint, we can tap into the positive liberty we crave. This moment of constraint, amid an endless cycle of action and reaction, releases us from a potentially egotistical and hedonistic lifestyle, from the domination of social pressure, and from the rat race of financial and societal advancement.

SURPASSING THE TYRANNY OF TECHNOLOGY

Today, we find many movements that call for a digital detox. Many people are searching for ways to liberate themselves from the dominance of the Internet and the pressures of consumerism. While so many search for a healthy escape route from modern-day burdens, Judaism has been practicing this ethic of deliberate rest for thousands of years. We call it "Shabbat," and when celebrated correctly, it offers the perfect therapy for the tyranny of technology.

The Jewish outlook has always refused to view modern society as essentially evil. Labor, creativity, and innovation are in fact indispensable elements of the destiny of man, as mandated in the Garden of Eden.[7] What becomes cursed is not labor but toil. Labor is a human's natural state; toil is the state we must learn to surpass. When celebrated properly, Shabbat

---

7. Genesis 2:15.

is a master class in the art of cultivating civilization. Rather than renouncing technology altogether, humans must attain some degree of independence from it. In doing so, we create an island in time and in space that redeems us from the vicissitudes of our toil. It is during this one day a week that humans reclaim dignity and reach beyond a basic work ethic to become enlightened to our true purpose on this earth.

SHABBAT: A TIME TO "BE"

Shabbat is not just a day to reacquaint ourselves with our positive freedom; it is also a day to return to a certain mode of existence that is often lost in the hustle and bustle of everyday life. This is the mode of existence that the German psychoanalyst Erich Fromm calls the mode of "being."[8] We have all too easily bought into a vision of society that worships materialism, one that confuses net worth with self-worth. Happiness is often pursued through the possession of expensive items. In fact, our definition of the self has sometimes become confined by what we have rather than who we are.

Amidst this material madness, are we still able to be alone with ourselves or get lost in our thoughts? Are we able to gaze out of the window when traveling a long distance and contemplate or marvel at our surroundings? Or do we instead busy ourselves with artificial noise and rapidly changing screens, in which we simultaneously lose ourselves and miss the opportunity of further finding ourselves? With all the good that social media has generated, there has unfortunately been a renewed emphasis on the very type of existence that Fromm warned against. The face-to-face encounter has been replaced with FaceTime and

---

8. Erich Fromm, *To Have or to Be?* (New York, 1976), 14–27.

Facebook, and the mode of "being" replaced by the mode of "having." Young people sometimes define their social status by how many friends they "have" on Snapchat, how many likes they "have" on Instagram, or how many followers they "have" on Twitter. The danger is clear. Without careful guidance, the "having" will become so overwhelming that we become totally enslaved to it, replacing the alternative mode of "being."

Fromm's message is more urgent today than ever before. He warns that if we continue as we are, we will only know how to relate to reality through the mode of "having," an existence where happiness, self-fulfillment, and inner peace are exclusively attained by acquiring things. Such an existence can lead to hedonism, envy, and greed. We need to re-engage with the mode of "being," an existence in which we are true to ourselves and seek real freedom through self-development in the intangibles of knowledge, happiness, love, and faith. Through this approach, we will find that we are able to experience the world around us rather than possessing it. To live in one extreme or the other reaps few benefits. What is required of us is to achieve a balance – to understand that the act of possessing is only one element of humanity. Indeed, it is an intrinsic part of our nature, and it occupies the majority of our time for six days a week. But if we want to nurture a society that values more than just materialism, we must also make space to experience "being" – an acquired art celebrated through Shabbat.

Shabbat creates the optimal conditions for us to face ourselves and assess our priorities, free from the noise of outside distractions. It reminds us of the importance of "time out" and the value of finding space for family, faith, and community. It allows us simply to be with ourselves and others without exacting a goal or a motive. It frees us from everything we are enslaved to during the week, enabling each of us to achieve our own personal exodus and emancipation. It allows us to enter the week refreshed, reenergized, and renewed, ready to assume our responsibilities to ourselves and to those around us. In that sense, Shabbat offers each of us the freedom to live as a human "being."

Two

Shabbat and the Soul

The History of Nature and the Nature of History

Where do we find spirituality? How can we connect to our soul, our spirit, and, ultimately, to the Divine? This nest of questions perplexes the modern individual, in constant pursuit of connection with something greater and more meaningful than his own mortality.

In the context of the physical and the material, the world has never been a more hospitable place for habitation. Across the globe, human beings are richer, freer, healthier, better-fed, and better-educated than ever before. Due to the relative scarcity of famine, drought, plagues, and major wars, the quality and length of our lives today outstrips every other era in history by a considerable margin.[1] Yet despite this, a phenomenon known as "hedonic adaptation" has begun to emerge.[2] We adjust to

---

1. These facts are demonstrated and explained at length by Steven Pinker, *Enlightenment Now* (New York, 2018).
2. Brickman and Campbell, "Hedonic relativism and planning the good society," in *Adaptation Level Theory: A Symposium* (Cambridge, 1971), 287–302.

a new normal, and aspects of life that were initially viewed as privileges become basic expectations. The fast-moving nature of modern life causes people to feel an increasing sense of angst if services are not provided at the unprecedented levels of efficiency. Commentators from almost every developed culture have noticed a precipitous decline in what might be called "spiritual well-being." Climbing rates of depression, loneliness, drug abuse, and anxiety can be observed everywhere. Levels of active participation in real social or professional associations have fallen across the Western world, as has participation in traditional communities. For far too many people, their popularity on social media is inversely proportional to the number of real-life friendships they enjoy. While the conditions of our physical existence seem to have significantly improved, we have somehow lost our internal tranquility and have destabilized the equilibrium of our souls. How can we remedy this situation? How can we carve out time to listen and tune into the spiritual music through the blaring cacophony of contemporary life?

A quick search through Jewish tradition reveals that two of the greatest medieval Jewish thinkers similarly wrestled with this question. Their ideological positions generate two major schools of thought, each advocating a different approach through which the individual may become attuned to the great spiritual power embedded within existence itself.

NATURE AND HISTORY

Maimonides – perhaps the greatest Jewish scholar, legalist, and scientist of the late medieval era – proposes that in order to effectively tap into the spirituality naturally embedded within the cosmos, one needs to contemplate creation itself. In Maimonides's worldview, through gazing up through a telescope or peering down through a microscope, through contemplating the astonishing, harmonious interdependence of nature's grand design, and through appreciating the brilliance of the grand Designer that lies behind the entire system, one's mind will inevitably be filled with feelings of awe, rapture, and spiritual inspiration.[3] In the past century, as our understanding of unified and immaculate natural laws has deepened, we have become able to commensurately extend our appreciation of the perfection of the Designer, and thus align our own minds to the Mind responsible for the magnificent interweaving of life itself. Such was the answer of this great medieval scientist and philosopher, who was able to discern the beauty and wisdom embedded within our broader environment. Although a tremendous challenge for the modern, harried individual, a deep understanding and appreciation of the world itself, through a lens of humility, remains the key ingredient for achieving spiritual tranquility.

The great medieval counterpart to Maimonides was the Arabian-Jewish poet and thinker Judah HaLevi. Many of his heart-rending compositions have made their way into our liturgy, and his literary-philosophical dialogue, known as the *Kuzari*, is one of the most engaging panoramic portrayals of the Jewish religion.[4] For HaLevi, there is a superior plane of human activity, beyond science and philosophy, that serves as a conduit for spiritual empowerment: the interaction between man and God in the arena of history.[5] For HaLevi, the

---

3. Maimonides, *Mishneh Torah, Hilkhot Yesodei HaTorah* 2:2.
4. Some of HaLevi's songs have been immortalized in Jewish liturgy. Examples include the Shabbat song "*Yom Shabbaton*" and the ballad of Jewish yearning "*Libi BaMizraḥ*."
5. *Kuzari*, 1:xiii–xxviii.

excruciating yet sublime trajectory of Jewish history, replete with triumphs and tragedies, returns and exiles, unparalleled achievements and unimaginable subjugation, constitutes the arena in which we may tune ourselves into the workings of the spiritual universe.

This perspective has gained additional momentum in our own century, in which the Jewish nation has stormed back onto the stage of history, rising from the ashes of destruction of the Holocaust to renew its sovereign existence in its ancient homeland. Our nation continues to wrestle with the challenges associated with power and self-determination on a daily basis. Those who have been fortunate enough to celebrate at the Western Wall on the commemoration of the reunification of Jerusalem or at sunrise on Shavuot will testify that it is difficult not to be swept up in feelings of national pride and spiritual elation. The exceptional events in our nation's history unite to form a wellspring of spirituality with which every sensitive soul can connect.

Maimonides, the scientist, seeks spirituality through contemplating the fixed regularities, the universal laws, and the ceaseless pendulum of the living world. HaLevi, the poet, seeks spirituality through the exceptional, the miraculous, and the uniqueness of the interaction between God and His people as manifested throughout human history. Practically, Maimonides's approach fosters an ethos of learning, of intellectual advancement, and the construction of a "scientific" form of Jewish theology and law. HaLevi's approach fosters an ethos of prayer, of introspection, and the patient cultivation of our unique inner spiritual proclivities. Maimonides' approach is universally accessible, HaLevi's is intensely particularistic. These two approaches represent two sides of the coin of Jewish theology, with a myriad of scholars subsequently developing each of these as distinct strains of thought.

How is it possible for an ordinary person to connect to these two conduits of spirituality? How can we tap into these resources through our mundane existence? How is the spiritual thirst quenched for one who may not be a scientist, poet, or philosopher? Fortunately, there is an institution – pivotal to the Jewish religious experience – that nurtures a spiritually attuned relationship to both nature and history: Shabbat.

UNITING THE HEMISPHERES OF OUR MIND

Indeed, these two avenues of spiritual enhancement are woven into the biblical depiction of Shabbat and expressed in the two citations of the Ten Commandments. In the first version, in the book of Exodus, Shabbat is portrayed as the climax of creation, the day upon which God ceased His frenetic activities and enjoyed a well-earned day of rest.[6] Following God's example, Shabbat is described as a weekly reenactment of this rest. We lay down our tools, turn off our devices, and tend to matters loftier than mere physical advancement. The biblical Sabbath is a day of truce, when we are forbidden from planting, reaping, sowing, digging, trapping, carrying, smoothing, repairing, or otherwise interfering with the natural order. So too we cease our war against nature. We refrain from manipulating any element of our environment; rather, we step back and reflect upon it. We appreciate and contemplate our place within the intricate cosmic order. Every week, we relate to nature not as an inexhaustible resource for personal and collective enrichment, but rather as a delicate system that reflects

---

6. Exodus 20:8–11.

the beneficence of an underlying spiritual equilibrium. We engage in the most basic of natural pleasures: eating, drinking, singing, conversing, resting, and learning. We take time to appreciate the quiet wonder of our world, thereby creating space to allow its humming spiritual beauty to enter into our lives.

Yet there is another side to Shabbat, woven into the second version of the Ten Commandments, that provides an entirely different rationale for Shabbat:

> Remember that you were a slave in the land of Egypt, and that the Lord your God has taken you out of there... therefore the Lord your God has commanded you to observe the Sabbath day.[7]

This is the other biblical aspect of Shabbat – the encounter of God and Human through great historical events. By resting from work on Shabbat, we commemorate how God has enabled us to enjoy these freedoms through His decisive historical intervention in freeing the Jewish nation from the crushing yoke of Egyptian tyranny. Shabbat is the sign of our continuous transcendence of the laws of history, in which small, scattered nations usually disappear into oblivion. Shabbat symbolizes the freedom that is enjoyed by all Jews, everywhere, regardless of circumstance: that inner freedom which stems from the knowledge that God has sealed a historical covenant with His people. The Jewish people have received a promise that – despite the temporary victory of our oppressors in every generation – there

---

7. Deuteronomy 5:12–15.

will be a restoration of our ultimate freedom and redemption in the future.[8]

The continued Jewish observance of Shabbat is the clearest demonstration of our historical faith and faith in history: just as God has overcome our previous oppressors, He will continue to intervene on our behalf, and lead our nation from darkness to light. Shabbat is a precious moment in time where we renew our relationship with the providential spirit that lies behind the magnificent history of the Jewish nation. We do this through commemorating the beginning – the Exodus from Egypt – and through anticipating the end – the Messianic Era, a time that rabbinic literature describes as a permanent, perfect Sabbath.[9]

Nature and history, intellect and emotion, universal laws and deep personal spiritual connections – these dichotomies find themselves expressed throughout Jewish tradition and are manifested in the duality at the heart of Shabbat. Shabbat is a day where we rejoin nature as partners, not as overlords. Shabbat is also a day where we contextualize ourselves within the grand Jewish story and prepare the world for the blissful climax of the historical process. Through these two paradigms, Shabbat calls upon us to halt the furious pace of our daily existence in order to open up these parallel pathways of spiritual enlightenment – allowing our souls to connect with the ultimate Source of spirituality and bring it into our daily lives.

---

8. This covenantal relationship and messianic promise is foreshadowed by the Covenant Between the Parts that cemented the relationship between God and Abraham; see Genesis 15:1–15.

9. Sanhedrin 97a.

Three

Shabbat and the Other
The Jewish Network

One of the great challenges of today's hyper-connected age is to form and maintain real relationships. Rather than investing in establishing strong bonds of mutual affinity and common purpose, it has become progressively easier to maintain relationships of convenience. There is a great temptation to hold onto hundreds of acquaintances at arm's length, maintaining a shallow or virtual connection to masses of individuals, and to call upon such "friendships" only when they appear useful to us. Moreover, as frantically busy human beings, we find little choice but to arrange for ourselves a hierarchy of friendships and relationships. In our own minds, we inadvertently ascribe importance to individuals based upon their utility to us, or even how much we want to find favor in their eyes. We often calibrate our social interactions not based upon an individual's worth as a person, but based upon our subjective desires or ambitions. Despite our own denials, all too often we view relationships with people as a means to a greater goal, rather than as ends in and of themselves.

22

Of course, most civilized people instinctively grasp the flawed nature of many modern relationships. We intellectually assent to the idea that all humans have a high intrinsic value and that we should endeavor to form meaningful connections with all the people within our sphere of influence. The demands of life, however, tend to prevent us from actualizing our ideals in this area. So, practically speaking, how may we improve ourselves? How can we take viable steps to reorient our perceptions in such a way that we form healthier, more meaningful relationships, and truly appreciate the intrinsic worth of every human being?

HIERARCHIES AND NETWORKS

One insight from contemporary academic scholarship may prove useful. As Harvard historian Niall Ferguson has described at length, our species is unique in our ability to organize ourselves via two very different types of social groupings: hierarchies and networks.[1] We are all familiar with hierarchies, where we organize ourselves in a top-down structure, with strong leaders (along with their acolytes) at the peak of the pyramid, controlling and organizing life for those in the lower social echelons. This structure is by far the most common in history, and, although it usually maintains order and stability within society, it survives by quashing the freedoms and aspirations of many who were expected to demonstrate unquestioned loyalty to the system. As such, hierarchies have been challenged by networks – loose affiliations of people acting of their own accord, without any overarching guidance

---

1. Niall Ferguson, *The Square and the Tower: Networks and Power, from the Freemasons to Facebook* (London, 2016).

from above, forming associations that are flexible and focused primarily on the individual's connections to peers. Such networks allow for greater expression of personal freedom. According to Ferguson, the Internet, global economy, technological innovation, business structures, governments, educational institutions, and even the military are abandoning the hierarchical model and leaning more towards operating according to networks, maximizing individual autonomy and thus collective productivity.

There is no doubt that living in a network age, which values the intrinsic importance of individual capabilities, entails tremendous advantages. The world is flatter, allowing people to branch out and operate in a less constrained manner, generating more money and connections than ever before. Yet, in our personal space, social hierarchies of importance and prestige still dominate. We revere certain people and disdain others. As previously mentioned, this sometimes leads us to develop friendships of convenience rather than investing in genuine relationships. In this context, how do we achieve the "network" effect on a more personal level? How can we attempt to dissolve our internal and judgmental hierarchies, and view people as an end in and of themselves? As is often the case, the Jewish tradition provides ancient yet surprisingly relevant answers to our quandary, one of which is Shabbat.

FROM THE BIBLE TO THE BOARDROOM

The book of Exodus introduces this theme through a thought-provoking narrative. The recently liberated Israelites, now encamped at Refidim, have received the divine manna, the heavenly proto-sustenance that descended daily upon their encampment in the wilderness. Moses, witnessing the double portion of Manna that falls on Friday, declares:

> A day of rest, a Holy Sabbath to the Lord is tomorrow. What you bake, bake, and what you cook, cook, and whatever is left over leave for yourselves... Eat it today, for today is a Sabbath day unto God, you shall not find it in the field.[2]

What is striking about the description in these verses is the definition of the Shabbat as a "day unto God" (*Shabbat hayom Lashem*). This perplexing phrase, which has been developed into a traditional song, requires some explanation. Surely, the monotheistic approach views all time and space as fundamentally belonging to God. What, then, is the meaning of this enigmatic description?

During this stage of the narrative, the primary focus of God's actions appears to be the transformation of a disputatious and traumatized throng of slaves into a unified and purpose-driven nation capable of internalizing and actualizing the Divine mission. Miracles are performed and certain laws (such as the introduction of the Hebrew calendar and the Paschal lamb)[3] are enacted toward this specific goal. Many events throughout the rest of the Torah narrative are indeed designed to strengthen the faith of the Israelites in their Redeemer, and to teach them to exercise their freedom through faithful service of God.

---

2. Exodus 16:23–30.
3. See for example Exodus 13–14.

Liberation, of a particular biblical sort, appears to be high on the agenda. No commandment is more emblematic of this paradigm shift than Shabbat.

The Israelites' slavery in Egypt and servitude to Pharaoh is a confirmation and perpetuation of the unyielding artificial hierarchy that existed in slave-owning societies. It represents an unassailable social order designed to increase the advantage of those of elite rank, to the perpetual misery and misfortune of the wretched classes at the bottom.

Until this point, the Israelites have been subject to toil without reprieve for the benefit of the privileged, without any hope of self-development or self-fulfillment. Service to God, as understood through the commandment of dedicating Shabbat as a "day unto God," constitutes a vigorous protest against the idolatrous megalomania of all despots, from Pharaoh's era until our own. Serving God is a mechanism that rejects human domination and replaces it with divine dominion, thereby encouraging the previously unimaginable idea that, at our most fundamental level, all human beings are equal.

LEVELING THE PLAYING FIELD

On Shabbat, all human hierarchical interests are declared illegitimate. Nobody is allowed to enrich themselves, promote their own social status, or utilize other human beings (or even animals, tools or machinery) to advance their own particular ends. People are enjoined to return to the *sanctum sanctorum* of their own homes, secure in the knowledge that the most important goods of life "shall not be found in the field."[4] God declares that on His day, He wishes to pause competition and advancement,

---

4. Ibid.

and promote free worship for free individuals. Shabbat is the day where we leave behind all forms of rigid hierarchy in our own lives and replace them with the largest, flattest, and most intensely egalitarian network that has ever been discovered by humankind: our radical equality before the majesty of God.

Following our biblical precedent, Judaism throughout history does not maintain a strenuous opposition to hierarchies as such, understanding them to be necessary for the stability of both the individual and the collective. However, it insists that there be a weekly relaxation within the hierarchical paradigm. We are instead encouraged to come together to form a community of prayer and learning, an association that recognizes no significant tribal or social stratification and promotes an anti-utilitarian conception of other human beings. The synagogue, one of the great Jewish inventions, serves as the gathering place for this communal network, where rich and poor, nobleman and nomad, all pray in undifferentiated unison.[5] In the house of prayer, we can enjoy a temporary cessation from social distinction and bask in the unconditional fraternity of all who have come to bare their hearts and souls in supplication.

A classic statement from one of the giants of Jewish thought neatly encapsulates the ethic of Shabbat as a social institution. Nahmanides – a prominent thirteenth-century rabbinic thinker, leader, physician, and commentator – considers the strangeness of placing Shabbat among the list of biblical festivals in Leviticus,[6] seeing as it does not share many of the external characteristics of a festival:

5. The synagogue in its current form was conceived as a response to the destruction of the Second Temple. For example, see Megilla 29a, where Rabbi Yitzhak interprets the "little sanctuaries" from Ezekiel 11:16 as synagogues.
6. Leviticus 23.

Indeed, the Sabbath is not truly one of the festivals. Nonetheless it is placed with them, and called a Holy Calling, because on this day all [of Israel] are enjoined to gather in sanctity. For it is a righteous deed for all of Israel to congregate in a synagogue on that day, to sanctify the day in public with prayers and rejoicing, to wear resplendent clothing, and to enact a day of feasting.[7]

The point of Shabbat is to gather all of Israel to the synagogue, regardless of age, gender, wealth, status, or affiliation. We are all called upon to rejoice, sing, and pray with one voice, to invite everyone to feast joyously, secure in the knowledge that we are being appreciated for who we are as individuals instead of how we may be useful to the aims of others. Shabbat is a day for ignoring all expectations and powerfully ingrained habits of socialization, to rejoice in the possibility of human freedom and equality, and to do our part to ensure that the entire community may partake of this weekly miracle.

To return to our original question: what can we introduce into our lives that will orient our mind towards cultivating deep relationships and treating people as ends in themselves? Shabbat. Go to synagogue with the mindset of merging with a larger community, of uniting with everyone in prayer and festivities. Invite strangers or distant acquaintances to break bread with your family and enjoy the prospect of entrenching new relationships. Finally, enjoy a day where we all stand together, as equals, before the great mystery and Master of life itself.

---

7. Nahmanides on Leviticus 23:1.

Four

Shabbat and Social Justice
Charitable Time

Albert Einstein summarized what he loved about Judaism as follows:

> The pursuit of knowledge for its own sake, *an almost fanatical love of justice*, and the desire for personal independence – these are the features of the Jewish tradition which make me thank my lucky stars that I belong to it.[1]

Deep in the recesses of our collective intellectual and religious heritage is an ancient Jewish concept called *tzedaka*. This concept is traditionally translated into English as "charity," yet it remains substantially different from the commonplace definition of that word. Judaism does not subscribe to the modern conception that helping someone in need is an act of pure charity, an effusion of altruistic goodness that goes above and beyond one's social duties. On the contrary, in the Hebrew

---

1. Albert Einstein, *The World As I See It* (New York, 1949), 47.

language, the word *tzedaka* derives its root from another crucial word: *tzedek*, or justice.

Assisting the vulnerable and the disadvantaged are acts that go beyond simple benevolence. Rather, they are fundamentally viewed as acts of justice. Every man and woman has a moral duty to rectify the wrongs within society, to ensure that all citizens – regardless of wealth or status – are able to live their lives with a basic level of dignity and self-respect. Using our physical resources to aid the vulnerable is not merely an act of generosity, but the fulfillment of a command, a divine obligation. This social and ethical obligation has informed Jewish practice throughout the centuries of our existence and continues to this day.

A PROTEST AGAINST INJUSTICE

It is indeed difficult, in the twenty-first century, to understand how revolutionary this attitude towards poverty is. For many centuries, much of the world understood poverty through one of two paradigms. The first is the Ancient Greek paradigm (a basic assumption of the political thought of both Plato and Aristotle) which sees human beings as irreversibly segregated into social classes, corresponding to the type or essence of that individual. If someone is born poor or a slave, then that is their rightful social station, from which they may never escape nor hope to elevate or ameliorate their situation. Some are simply born to rule and others are born to be ruled. The other paradigm is heavily influenced by Christian ideology and sees impoverishment as a blessed state, in which the hardships endured in the physical world will surely stand an individual in good stead to be accepted in the Kingdom of Heaven. Poverty is a sign of divine blessing and is simply to be endured until the meek inherit the earth.

Although these two ideas have been fashionable for much of world history, Judaism categorically rejects both. Poverty and deprivation are never to be romanticized. They are a curse, to be fought against by all means possible. There are dozens of biblical passages requiring individuals to donate a significant portion of their wealth to "the stranger, the orphan, the widow..."[2] Later rabbinic laws continued in this spirit of collective social responsibility, to the extent that Maimonides, the greatest Jewish legal authority of the medieval period, could state that "We have neither heard nor seen of a Jewish community that does not have a fund for the needy."[3]

This idea of a societal safety net for the disadvantaged – introduced into Western countries as late as the twentieth century – is woven into the Jewish calendar and life cycle through two central institutions that mirror each other in both structure and content: *Shemitta* (the sabbatical year where fields are left fallow) and Shabbat (the sabbatical day).

RESTING AS SOCIAL JUSTICE

These two sets of laws are intertwined in the biblical chapter listing the civil laws that delineate the interpersonal relationships between individual members of the Jewish nation:

> Six years you shall sow the land and gather its produce.
> But in the seventh you shall let it go and let it lie fallow,
> and your people's indigent may eat of it... Six days you
> shall do your deeds and on the seventh day you shall

---

2. Deuteronomy 10:18, for example.
3. Maimonides, *Hilkhot Mattenot Aniyyim* 9:3.

> cease, so that your ox and donkey may rest, and your
> bondman and the sojourner catch their breath.[4]

The parallels between Shabbat and *Shemitta* are immediately apparent – they both occur at the end of their respective cycle of seven units, they both involve an absolute cessation of work, and the rationale given in these verses for both commandments includes caring for the disadvantaged of society (as well as the domestic animals of the Israelites). It is in this context that the institutions of both Shabbat and *Shemitta* are introduced to further enhance the ethic of social justice.

One of the most pressing conundrums in the history of political philosophy involves the attempt to balance two cardinal values of human interaction. On the one hand, we wish to preserve the right to advance one's own socio-economic situation untrammeled by external interference, while, on the other hand, we recognize the humanitarian imperative of closing the ever-widening gap between the wealthiest and neediest elements of society. The capitalist paradigm overemphasizes the former, whereas the socialist ideal attempts to coerce the latter. The solution proposed through the biblical institutions of Shabbat and *Shemitta* is simultaneously more subtle and more provocative than either of these economic approaches.

The Bible, while encouraging assiduous labor and the accumulation of wealth, nevertheless instills within Jewish society a mechanism by which each citizen is periodically reminded of the transience of their ownership over property. Every week, we are forced to confront the reality that

---

4. Exodus 23:10–13.

everything we imagine to be under our governance, including our workers and domestic animals, does not, in fact, belong to us in any meaningful sense. We cannot work, manipulate, benefit from, or demonstrate any other manner of ownership over these dependents. Imbued within the Jewish calendar is a weekly reminder that no matter how much material capital we accrue, there is a higher reality that encompasses all of God's creatures, a reality where wealth, rank, and status are declared irrelevant.

The ethic of *Shemitta* is an extended manifestation of the same principle as Shabbat, reinforcing this same ethic of social responsibility. One's field, the pinnacle of economic dependability in an agrarian society, is utterly untouchable for an entire year. It is to be forsaken in its entirety, and its gates are to be thrown open to the disadvantaged who will enjoy unhindered access for the duration of the year. For any proud farmer, there can be no more obvious demonstration of the ephemeral nature of his or her tenure than to witness the local indigent assuming provisional ownership of the farmer's prized ancestral domain. To observe *Shemitta* is to declare that our own material possessions are bestowed upon us in order that we may share God's blessing.

Shabbat and *Shemitta* are indeed cornerstones of the biblical notion of social justice. Through experiencing these sevenfold cycles of time that demand periods of abstinence from commonplace acts of possession, Jews are regularly forced to confront the painful transience of their entire concept of possession. We do not truly own our possessions – we are merely custodians of God's blessings, bestowed upon us on condition that we allow others to partake. We are therefore encouraged to utilize these transient possessions for the loftier aim of alleviating the crushing yoke of poverty and preserving the dignity of the disadvantaged. This religiously mandated weekly shift in consciousness from ownership to custodianship, from a materialistic ethic of domination to spiritually oriented ambitions of benevolence, lies at the core of the Jewish ambition to create a society in which poverty and deprivation are mere relics of the past.

After millennia of observing Shabbat and *Shemitta*, are we not greatly sensitized to the cry of others? With this ethical principle hardwired into our historical psyche, is it any wonder that so many Jews have lifted their eyes beyond their own horizons and taken up the cause of the poor and the oppressed across the entire world?

SENSITIZING OURSELVES TO AND THROUGH THE NEEDS OF OTHERS

One might be tempted to ask, however, how one may practically adapt this ethos in the twenty-first century. After all, very few of us own servants or donkeys, and we certainly don't own a field that we may throw open to the poor. Nonetheless, Shabbat still serves as a focal point of our social responsibility within our own community. Charity as justice starts at home.[5] We could open our hearts and take it upon ourselves to ensure that no Jewish family is without the means to put food on their Shabbat table, through supporting the numerous charities across the globe that work to provide weekly support to Jews in need. We could open our synagogues and encourage all Jews to attend our social and religious events, to draw those who dwell on the

---

5. The talmudic expression for this principle is "The poor of your own city take precedence" (Bava Metzia 71a).

periphery of our community in to enjoy the warmth and mutual support of an inclusive Jewish environment. We could open our homes and invite all those in desperate need of friendship and a good meal to join our families as we celebrate the wonderful blessings that God has bestowed upon us.

If we are able to internalize this message of Shabbat and provide genuine Jewish care for the world's vulnerable and disadvantaged, then surely we will have taken a step in the right direction towards fulfilling our mandate of bringing down God's blessing into our world.

Five

Shabbat and Our Humanity

Placing Limits to Achieve the Limitless

What makes us human? How do we distinguish ourselves from the animal kingdom? This question constitutes the basis of one of the most intriguing scientific and philosophical debates of the last century. At the heart of the human condition lies an unbridgeable chasm that separates between the two elements that comprise our humanity.

On the one hand, modern science has informed us that – on a physical level – we are extremely close to our animal kin. Only half a chromosome away from a chimpanzee, human beings display many of the basic drives, needs, and fears that render us almost identical to our mammalian cousins. We seldom admit to ourselves the uncomfortable truth about how much of our lives are spent worrying about, and responding to, our most primal requirements. However, while the animalistic side of humankind is abundantly clear, we are also confronted by our staggering uniqueness and ability to transcend the animal within.

Scientific and technological advancements have allowed us to dominate the earth to an unimaginable degree, and our cultural, intellectual, and artistic achievements reflect an emotional and imaginative dimension that has no parallel in the natural world. Both sides of the human narrative may be experienced when reading a great novel; one can either be disappointed at the human frailties and weaknesses that motivate the characters, or marvel at the exquisite artistry of the novelist in their portrayal of the human condition.

In short, we are caught between the characteristics that have been granted to us by our natural origins and the sublime, noble characteristics that the Bible calls "the image of God."[1] This dual conception raises a practical dilemma. On the one hand, we humans have acquired a phenomenal understanding of the workings of the world, and on the other hand, we seem somewhat unsure how best to utilize this tremendous gift: Do we develop better medicines or more efficient nuclear weapons? Should we chase higher profit margins or work to lower rates of poverty? With such power and knowledge at our disposal, how can we ensure that we live up to our humanity? How do we prevent ourselves from becoming paralyzed by the overwhelming potential good contained within each decision we make? Marianne Williamson famously wrote that, "Our deepest fear is not that we are inadequate. Our deepest fear is that we are powerful beyond measure. It is our light, not our darkness, that most frightens us."[2] What practical steps may we undertake to maintain close control over our animal instincts and overcome

---

1. Genesis 1:26–27.
2. Marianne Williamson, *A Return To Love: Reflections on the Principles of a Course in Miracles* (New York, 1992), 190–191.

the fear of allowing the more exquisite, humane side of our species to develop?

RECOGNIZING STRENGTHS AND WEAKNESSES

One approach involves the early recognition of our human weaknesses and the subsequent placing of limits upon our own behavior. Before we are faced with urgent ethical dilemmas (in which we may fall prey to our own frailties), we must undertake due diligence in outlining the acceptable limits of human behavior. Historically, of course, this is a relatively recent realization. It was only in the nineteenth century that the civilized nations of the world outlawed slavery (the temptation to subjugate other human beings to our personal desires), and only subsequently did society gradually follow it up with the ethical prohibitions against cruelty to animals, torture of prisoners, exploitation of children, proliferation of nuclear weaponry, and human cloning.

Most nations have made it a priority to compose a national constitution that places precise limits upon the scope of governmental power, ostensibly ensuring democratic freedoms for all citizens. Human beings are at their best when they are able to impose strict limits upon their behavior based on a recognition of their limitations and proscribe practices to a degree that is commensurate with our dignity as a species. As such, conquering ourselves is the key to remaining true to ourselves. This need to conquer ourselves and to control our otherwise animalistic instincts in order to live a more humane life is a running motif throughout Jewish religious literature. In one of the most outstandingly counterintuitive and yet relevant sources in ancient Judaism, the Mishna quotes the second-century sage Shimon ben Zoma as dispensing the following advice:

> Who is a wise person? One who learns from every person.
> Who is a strong person? One who conquers their own desires.
> Who is a rich person? One who is happy with their lot.
> Who is an honorable person? One who honors others.[3]

Although written in an individual vein, this jarring and poetic Mishna exemplifies the theme of establishing personal limitations as key to moral excellence. The key to wisdom, as Socrates also notes, is knowing the limits of our own intellects and thus making space in our minds to listen to others. The key to strength is recognizing our own weaknesses and working to overcome them, just as the key to wealth is through the recognition that it does not depend on financial capital alone, but also on inner serenity and contentment. Finally, the moment that a person knows how to constrain their self-importance enough to honor their fellow creatures is the moment that they are truly worthy of honor themselves.

Judaism is a religion that keenly understands the struggle with this dilemma that is at the heart of our humanity. One of the great Jewish thinkers of the twentieth century, Rabbi Joseph B. Soloveitchik, tackles this dual nature of humanity in his

---

3. Ethics of the Fathers 4:1.

classic essay "Majesty and Humility."[4] He claims that much of Jewish traditional practice may be understood in the light of our attempt to satisfy our physical instincts on the one hand, yet cultivate our elevated and edifying human traits on the other. The Jewish solution, according to Rabbi Soloveitchik, is to mandate an approach to life that encourages an ethic of "conquest-and-retreat," encouraging our human desires to a considerable degree – yet bridling them through pre-arranged limitations, thereby allowing space for our humane side to develop and sanctify itself.

To this purpose, Judaism encourages people to make as much money as they desire – yet mandates that they give at least ten percent of it to charity, enjoining us to care for the vulnerable members of our society. Judaism appreciates beauty and physical attraction, yet imposes an ethic of *tzniut* (modesty) upon men and women alike. This allows us to rise above the pitfalls of vanity and lust and appreciate individuals for their character and personality, not merely their physical appearance. Judaism encourages a robust amount of festive dining and drinking – yet requires that the food be prepared in a specific way, that blessings be recited before and after consumption, and that the conversation be dignified. *Halakha* (Jewish law) allows us to respond to our physical appetites in the short-term, yet ensures that we are not overtaken by them. It creates space in our minds to rationally consider how we may best calibrate our actions with the better angels of our nature. Of course, we are partially animals – but humanity would be impoverished indeed if we allowed ourselves to be entirely defined by our lower instincts.

---

4. Rabbi Joseph B. Soloveitchik, *Confrontation and Other Essays* (Maggid, 2015), 25–40.

PART OF NATURE – YET APART FROM IT

The most sustained and powerful of these restraining techniques is, of course, the Shabbat.

Hard work and mastery over nature is certainly encouraged in the Bible: "Six days you shall engage in work."[5] For six days a week, humans are encouraged to pursue that most elusive and treasured of goals: material success. This pursuit is a primary motivating factor within human life and must be respected. Yet we must also appreciate that success can become utterly intoxicating, and therefore we must take great care to place limits upon it. Success is such a tantalizing prospect that it has the ability to secure an iron grip on our attention, to the point that our animalistic side can take over and we feel we have no choice but to make it the primary priority of our investment. We should know better. In our heart of hearts, we acknowledge that the truly important values, the truly precious moments, and the truly worthwhile endeavors are rarely intertwined with the pursuit of personal success.

As such, constraining the obsessive pursuit of personal success in a manner that is productive and vivifying should be a priority for all who desire to rise above common distractions and pursue a truly edified life. Across the globe, millions of hardworking Jews set down their work tools on Friday evening and embark upon a full day of mental, emotional, intellectual, and spiritual rejuvenation. In the process they rediscover some astonishing things. They rediscover – contrary to stoked egos – that the furious-paced worlds of business, media, and news cycles manage perfectly well without them. They rediscover the manifold benefits of long hours of peace and tranquility. They

---

5. Exodus 35:2.

rediscover the delights of spending significant time with family who do not always receive enough attention during the week. They rediscover the pleasures of worshipping with friends and strangers in the synagogue, of fine dining, of extended face-to-face human contact, and of learning words of wisdom. Most importantly, they entrench in their mind the rarely acknowledged fact that there are things in life that matter far more than our hedonistic desires would like us to acknowledge. There are things of genuine, irreducible, irreplaceable, transcendental importance. Can those who ignore such truths truly live a meaningful life?

Shabbat is a brilliant invention for many reasons. Perhaps the most important, however, is that it places a much-needed limit upon our self-centered desire to climb the social or financial ladder. It is a mandatory pause for breath. It is a rare, precious opportunity to leave behind the messy, contentious world of physical advancement and cultivate the delicate flower of our sublime humanity.

Six

Shabbat and the Jewish Revolution

Timeliness and Timelessness

The Jewish people have a special relationship with time.

For thousands of years, Judaism has rotated around the axis of a fixed calendar through the ascription of ceremonial and commemorative moments. This calendar, which synthesizes a sensitivity towards both seasonal cycles and historical events, has a remarkable impact on the lifestyle of its adherents. It mandates days for mourning, days for feasting, days of levity, and days of seriousness, and extended periods may be spent either in intense introspection or joyous anticipation. It is a system that encourages a remarkable spectrum of emotional, intellectual, and historical sensitivities, lending a cathartic wholeness to the year. The message of such a lifestyle is that God is principally available in the realm of time, where the rituals and exigencies of the lunar calendar transform the solar year into a religious journey, a series of temporal rendezvous with the Divine.

Fittingly, the very first commandment that the Israelites were given upon being released from slavery in Egypt was that of formulating a reliable calendar, so that the peaks and troughs of religious experience may be incorporated into Jewish living.[1] For the most basic attribute of national independence is the ability to form a calendar that underscores the rhythm of our own particular national and religious life.

Shabbat, however, is an outlier. Unlike any other unit of time within our calendar (days, months, and years), the week is not designed to be commensurate to any particular astronomical event. As it commemorates the original, seven-day blueprint that fashioned the universe, the weekly structure is as ceaseless and imperiously unwavering as the universe itself. In the same vein, Shabbat is not overridden by any other calendrical event, no matter how joyful or somber. Shabbat stands alone, irreplaceable and untouchable, with its customs, laws, and ceremonies continuing largely unabated regardless of circumstance.

A FIXED ANCHOR IN THE STORM OF HISTORY

Historically, this consistency has been crucial to the Jewish experience, symbolizing the unbreakable relationship between God and His people, a relationship that transcends all transitory events and seasons. Throughout the entire awe-inspiring tapestry of Jewish history, Shabbat has constituted an anchor of stability and transcendence. For millennia, every single week without failure, Jews have stepped aside from their trials and tribulations in order to celebrate. The seignior languishing in King David's ancient palace, the fugitive fleeing persecution by the Inquisition, the desperate fighter in the Warsaw Ghetto,

---

1. Exodus 12:2.

and the hedge fund manager escaping the relentlessness of Wall Street have all shared this weekly encounter with the Divine. That any Jew, in any circumstance, could be transformed each week from a pauper into a prince, from a pariah into a lover, provides the Jewish nation with an unparalleled wellspring of moral, spiritual, and psychological strength. Ahad Ha'am, one of the greatest of the early Zionist thinkers and essayists, memorably states: "More than the Jews have kept the Sabbath, the Sabbath has kept the Jews."[2]

The Jewish attitude towards time, however, is not merely a reflection of our own internal life cycle. Rather, it is an indelible element of the "Jewish revolution" that has changed the face of humanity forever. To understand the source of this, one must embark on a fascinating comparison between two Biblical institutions within the book of Exodus: The *Mishkan* (Tabernacle) and Shabbat.

The closing fifteen chapters of the book of Exodus constitute an independent unit, a combination of narrative and legal sections. Beginning in chapter 25, we have a lengthy section outlining the construction of the *Mishkan*, the tabernacle that the Israelites are commanded to build in the wilderness to house the Lord. In chapter 31, there is a diversion as the commandment of Shabbat is given to the Israelites. Following the episode of the Israelites' national betrayal with the Golden Calf, there is an additional reminder of the laws of Shabbat, followed by several chapters further chronicling the construction of the *Mishkan* that conclude the book of Exodus. This cyclical, chiastic structure (*Mishkan*-Shabbat-Narrative-Shabbat-*Mishkan*)

---

2. Ahad Ha'am, *Ten Essays on Zionism and Judaism* (New York, 1973).

has been noted and commented upon throughout the centuries and requires explanation.

The Talmud observes this relationship and states that the work of building the *Mishkan* is suspended on Shabbat, demonstrating the latter's supremacy.[3] Furthermore, all thirty-nine primary categories of prohibitions of Shabbat are extrapolated by the Rabbis from the thirty-nine types of physical labor that was necessitated for building the *Mishkan*.[4] The *Mishkan* and Shabbat both represent the epitome of holiness, of the ability of mortals to somehow relate to, and commune with, the Divine, with one representation operating through the dimension of space (*Mishkan*) and the other through the dimension of time (Shabbat).

JUDAISM'S GREATEST GIFT

An essential element of the pagan worldview is the elevation and worship of entities in the realm of physical space – a tree, a mountain, a statue, a temple, even a human. All these, however, may be created or destroyed, edified or denigrated and, most importantly, owned or manipulated by human beings. Indeed, the history of idolatry is the history of certain religious castes claiming superior knowledge and dominion over specific holy places or objects. This spatial centralization of holiness and power allowed for the sublimation of such deities to the whims and ambitions of their supposed adherents.

The first and most impactful gift of Judaism to the world is that of monotheism – a worldview that does not allow for the monopolization of holiness. God – the only

---

3. Yevamot 6a.
4. Shabbat 49a.

being worthy of worship – exists everywhere and can therefore be worshipped from anywhere by anyone. Although certain defined spaces (such as the Land of Israel) may enjoy a greater concentration of Divine presence, His existence suffuses all.

Space is particularistic. Time, on the other hand, is universal. This universalization of God is the first of many revolutionary ideas of the Hebrew Bible and resonates unto this day. The ethical implication of this idea is staggering. God's constant presence, and the eternal expectations that He has placed upon humanity, create a universal standard of moral behavior. He cannot be bought or bribed, supplicated or placated merely with sacrifices and prayer. It matters not whether or not one is "chosen" – mere status as a human being demands that we live up to divine expectations and creates a similar demand that all others treat us as divine beings worthy of respect.

The association of God with time removes Him from the manipulations of other human beings who could claim ownership of specific holy objects or places. He is above spatial concerns; He is above all the minutiae of geopolitical squabbles and petty confrontations relating to control of space. Since all living beings have equal access to the realm of time, it follows that all may consider themselves as having equal access to the Divine Presence that animates it.

The most striking example of this principle is the primacy, both chronologically and ideologically, of Shabbat. The very first entity to be sanctified in the Bible is the Shabbat. After creating an infinite expanse of spatial objects, God noticeably abstains from setting any of them apart as holy. Instead, He chooses to sanctify a specific day as the primary medium through which holiness is to be experienced. Indeed, at Mount Sinai, God sets apart a particular people as a holy nation. And it is only after witnessing the primitive need of this people to have an object of worship in their midst (as displayed by the savagery and revelry that characterizes the episode of the Golden Calf)[5] that the *Mishkan* is erected and sanctified. However, even as the *Mishkan* is being built, with all the magnificent creativity and religious devotion that accompanies it, the principle of the Shabbat is repeatedly reinforced. The attentive listener may just hear the text as it whispers its most basic religious principle: *Don't imagine that God only resides in a place, but also in time. Don't forget the universal reach of God: Remember the Sabbath and keep it holy.*

When we make Shabbat a central part of our lives, we are bearing witness and pledging allegiance to some of the most foundational beliefs that the Jews have bequeathed to humankind. We affirm the belief that God is accessible within the realm of time, and therefore every being may reach out to Him at any time, in any place and during any circumstance. We affirm the idea that all of us humans can and must internalize the constant Divine Presence in our lives and should strive to calibrate our behavior to a standard that behooves our Godly origins.

Most importantly, however, we affirm our connection to eternity. Just as God is ultimately above time (as the ceaseless regularity of the Shabbat reminds us), He has bestowed upon human beings certain capacities that allow us too to transcend time. Inasmuch as we are mere animalistic beings, we are indeed subject to time and death. As human beings

---

5. Exodus 22.

created in the image of God, however, we are endowed with a soul, with the capability for reason, choice, love, and freedom beyond expressing specific emotions at fixed times prescribed by the calendar. This Godly awareness gives us the tools to transcend our existence as mere physical beings and, in a sense, achieve immortality.

Celebrating the beauty and holiness of Shabbat is a declaration of loyalty to the great gifts that the Jewish people have bestowed upon mankind, and a statement of hope for the day when we may witness every human being connect to God with love and freedom.

Seven

Shabbat and the Messiah

A Preview of Eternity

Shabbat is our weekly preview of Utopia. Ever since its inception, Shabbat has been closely linked with an immensely influential idea that is one of the core beliefs of Judaism: that the struggles and setbacks of history will come to an end, and humankind will enjoy an era of prosperity, tranquility, and spiritual fulfillment. This vision constitutes the final, irreversible victory of peace over war, equality over oppression, and spiritual bliss over physical drudgery. In this eschatological future, the nation of Israel will coalesce in the Promised Land and invite the nations of the world to join them in the service of God and the pursuit of enlightened wisdom. We usually refer to this state of affairs as "the coming of the *Mashiaḥ* (Messiah)" and it is best characterized by the verse in Isaiah, "Nation shall not lift up sword unto other nations, nor shall they learn warfare anymore."[1]

---

1. Isaiah 2:4.

OUR UNIQUE VISION

While the broad messianic idea is indeed shared by many cultures and religions, the Jewish vision of the Messiah is unique in several significant ways. Other major religions conceive of redemption as dependent entirely upon the grace of God, who must bestow redemption upon a fatally flawed and tragically fallen humankind.[2] The Jewish view, however, is entirely different. As the Talmud points out, the Jewish nation must *earn* their redemption through repentance, loyalty, and good deeds.[3] This notion lends immense strength and endurance to the long-suffering Jewish nation, who believe that it is down to every individual and every generation to force God's hand, so to speak – to perfect themselves and the world to such a degree that the world becomes a receptacle for the Divine Presence Itself. This would help explain why the belief in the Messiah is considered a fundamental tenet of Judaism, the denial of which is tantamount to heresy.[4] The belief in the Messiah is, in fact, a radical belief in ourselves and our ability to bring redemption to the world through self-improvement and the pursuit of justice and kindness. This attitude constitutes the very core of the entire worldview of Judaism.

The messianic idea gives rise to a wonderfully optimistic view of humankind. We do not believe that human beings are tainted by some sort of original sin, nor imbued with weaknesses and vulnerabilities that cannot be overcome. Nor do we presume that we need divine grace in order to lead ethical

---

2. Meir Soloveitchik, "Redemption and the Power of Man," *Azure* 16 (Winter 2004).
3. Sanhedrin 97b.
4. Maimonides, *Mishneh Torah, Hilkhot Melakhim UMilḥemoteihem* 11:4.

lives. On the contrary – our role on this earth is precisely to overcome our frailties, to exert tremendous effort in forging a path of holiness and decency that will shine as a beacon of light in a sometimes dark and treacherous world. Although imperfect, we are far from helpless. Affirming the coming of the Messiah is an affirmation of the fundamental goodness of humanity and an affirmation of the wisdom of the One who took the momentous decision to create humankind in His own image, capable of choosing good over evil.

So how do we prepare ourselves for the coming of the Messiah? How do we entrench in our minds the notion that we have an obligation to take small, steady, incremental steps to perfect the world?

LEARNING THROUGH IMMERSION

Already thousands of years ago, the Jewish faith (as well as other faiths) grasped an educational principle that is only now beginning to be appreciated across the world. From its very inception, Judaism appreciates that in order to ingrain ideas and values into people's minds, *active participation* is essential. A visceral, synesthetic, immersive experience remains lodged in the memory long after declarations and resolutions have faded into dust. Anyone who has witnessed a Seder night, where Jewish families sit together to recount the Exodus from Egypt, is always struck by the elaborate and immersive nature of the rituals: Matza is broken into two, wine is drunk, songs are sung, the door is opened, stories are told, children are questioned, vegetables are dipped in salt water. Ideas are entrenched in the mind, and etched on the soul, through moving, hearing, ingesting, and engaging. Similarly, on the fast of the ninth of Av, we quite literally sit on the floor and abstain from eating or socializing in order to feel the grave loss of our national homeland. When we dip our bodies in the purifying water of the *mikve*, we don't merely become pure on a technical level – we immerse our entire being in order to *experience* the purity and cleanliness in all our limbs. Therefore, when we wish to inculcate within ourselves the importance and urgency of the messianic idea, we turn to one ancient experiential institution: Shabbat.

Shabbat is a day where we are commanded to create for ourselves a brief immersive preview of this messianic future by stopping all toil and focusing on the loftiest elements of human existence. As Rabbi Jonathan Sacks states, "The Shabbat is not simply a day of rest. It is an anticipation of 'the end of history,' the Messianic Age. On it, we recover the lost harmonies of the Garden of Eden."[5]

Our observance of Shabbat encapsulates our beliefs about humanity's ability to perfect the world. The hallmark of a Shabbat properly observed is the unique spirit of holiness and tranquility that fills the void we create by ceasing all work – it is that brief moment of eternity, of harmony, of perfection, that we carve out in our own lives every week.

A weekly dress rehearsal for the Messianic Age seems to be a very ambitious project for mere mortals, and the question naturally arises as to how we are supposed to understand, let alone achieve, this small miracle. Indeed, there is no perfectly clear picture within Jewish sources as to the precise nature of the Messianic Era, and to what extent the world will change from what it is today. Some mysteries are beyond human comprehension, at least for the time being. However, as the great

5. Jonathan Sacks, "The Sabbath: First Day or Last?" *Covenant and Conversation*, March 13, 2017.

scholar of Jewish mysticism Gershom Scholem explores at
length, there is a central tension within the Jewish tradition
regarding the Messiah.[6] Two schools of thought have placed
an emphasis upon different facets of the Messianic Era, based
upon different ways of reading the prophetic visions of the
end of days found in the biblical books of Isaiah, Malachi,
and Zechariah.

On the one hand, the *literalist* approach takes the grand
messianic prophecies at face value, and emphasizes that the
Messianic Age will constitute a radical break from the kind of
existence that we experience in our current lives.[7] This school
of thought understands that our world will undergo a radical transformation. Miracles will abound, as God's immedi-
ate presence will overwhelm the natural order. Both human
civilization and the animal kingdom will become places of
benign coexistence and joyous harmony. There will be an over-
abundance of natural resources, to the extent that no sentient
creature will experience any deficiency. Most importantly, all
the painful elements of human existence, including infirmity,
disease, and even death itself, will eventually be eradicated
from the earth.

On the other hand, the *metaphorical* approach pres-
ents a more cautious, familiar, naturalistic vision of the end
of days.[8] According to this view, nature itself will not undergo
any radical transformation, nor will there be a surfeit of open
miracles. People will still die, and animals will still consume
each other. However, the Jewish people will lead a strong and

---

6. Gershom Scholem, *The Messianic Idea in Judaism* (New York, 1971), 1–36.
7. For instance, see Nahmanides on Leviticus 26:6.
8. For instance, see Maimonides, *Hilkhot Melakhim UMilḥemoteihem* 12.

safe existence in their own homeland and the entire world will coalesce together in a recognition of God's glory. Human beings will cease to cause irreparable damage to each other and to the environment, as all nations will resolve to permanently end strife, warfare, and poverty. All will pursue wisdom and virtue instead of power and wealth. In this utopian vision, we will all lead the best human life possible – but it will still be a fundamentally *human* life.

PURSUING OUR BEST SELVES

Of course, it is impossible for us to know for certain exactly which of these schools of thought portray the more accurate picture. However, the Jewish ideal strives to emphasize the importance of incorporating both visions into our own messianic ideals – embracing both the natural and the supernatural. We eagerly await the day that open miracles will reveal God's presence and end all sorrow – yet at the same time, we actively work towards the day that humanity will unite to pursue a global agenda of peace, friendship, and righteousness. Our messianic yearnings combine the possibility of supreme divine presence with the urgent imperative of repairing the world through moral courage and relentless self-improvement.

As a prelude to the Messianic Era, Shabbat must contain the seeds of both of these religious ambitions. On the one hand, we strive – through human effort and meticulous preparation – to create a Shabbat experience that serves as a microcosm of a fairer, simpler, loftier, more beautiful and harmonious world. We attempt to create a day that will exemplify all the greatest human virtues and habits: resting from work, creating a warm communal environment, welcoming strangers and guests into our home, spending time with family, appreciating fine food and drink, and reading words of wisdom. We do all that we can to make peace with ourselves and with our fellows. At the same time, we also do all that we can to make peace with God Himself. Shabbat is a day in which we reach upwards and invite the divine spark into our lives. We go to the synagogue to pray in elaborate services. We sing heartfelt songs and poems to honor the Shabbat day. We pause our noisy and overwhelming lives in order to just sit, meditate, and listen to the awesome silence, through which we can faintly sense the presence of something greater and more meaningful than anything else we had envisioned. We reach out to God, in an honest attempt to repair a relationship that all too often gets trampled in our rush to keep up with life. And in this experiential and immersive manner, every Shabbat, we demonstrate to ourselves the way in which we usher in a Messianic Era step by step – first through repairing the human world, and then through connecting ourselves with the Divine.

This, perhaps, is the highest form of observing Shabbat: the creation of a day in which we may live, however temporarily, in the shadow of the Messiah. Maimonides, the great medieval sage, sums up the Jewish messianic dream as follows:

> At that time there will be no famine and no war, no envy and no strife, for the Good will pervade everything. And all the delights of the world will be as readily available as dust. The world will be engaged only with communing with God… and they will achieve a communion with God to the highest degree that is humanly possible.[9]

---

9. Maimonides, *Hilkhot Melakhim UMilḥemoteihem* 12:5.

World peace, universal contentment, and the highest form of spiritual connection. Is there a more elevated vision than this? Through experiencing the Shabbat, we may prepare ourselves, our families, our communities, and subsequently the entire world for such a vision.

The Invention of Experiential Education

When we open our computers, we are hardly surprised to find that we have left multiple Internet browsers open. This habit represents a microcosm of the mindset of the modern, efficient, multitasking individual: many different aspects, different foci, blend seamlessly together as we flick from one screen to another and back again. This image parallels the varied, overlapping elements of our identities.

Our lives are not one homogenous unit, but rather comprise multiple elements that constitute the self. Our inner psyche, our habits and behaviors, our thoughts and ambitions, our religious and ideological worldviews, our relationships with family and friends, our social expectations and practices, our cultural heritage, and our spiritual strivings all contribute to the great amalgamation that we call life. As with multiple browsers open on our computer, different facets of our selves receive greater amounts of attention at different points of our lives, as our priorities, passions, and time pressures constantly shift. Yet the wise individual is aware of the ineradicable presence of all these different elements, and the imperative of tending to the unique needs of every facet of our lives. Only through this awareness may a person hope to achieve inner equilibrium.

Shabbat, an institution with several millennia of wisdom and experience behind it, is simply unparalleled in its ability to cultivate and nurture a wide array of elements that are essential to the multifaceted experience that is the human condition. When preserved and protected, Shabbat constitutes the vehicle through which transformative waves of meaning are transmitted from the inner core of our souls, to our daily lives, to our families and communities, and – finally – to humanity as a whole.

As described throughout this work, celebrating the true essence of Shabbat revolutionizes the notion of rest into a complete and enriching experience of restoration, enabling us to reunite with our core sense of self and identity. We rejuvenate our souls, recalibrate our minds towards our true purpose, regain perspective on our journey of self-discovery, and reassess our priorities free from the noise of outside distractions. On this unique day, we are counterintuitively shown that the ultimate moment of creativity can be found in the momentary suspension of creative activity, and we experience the true freedom of positive liberty in the process.

I have shared a glimpse into how Shabbat calls upon us to halt the furious pace of our daily existence in order to allow our souls to reconnect with the natural order, with our place within the universal historical progression, and ultimately with Divinity itself. It is a precious moment in time, during which all hierarchical interests are set aside, where we coalesce as a unified community that sings, prays, and pursues righteousness as one. We recall and celebrate the inherent value of each individual regardless of societal class or stature. The mandatory pause in our frantic pursuit of success that is imposed by Shabbat enables us to focus our attention upon those less fortunate than ourselves and pursue the uniquely Jewish form of justice through our compassion for society's marginalized and vulnerable populations. Shabbat confers this rare and precious opportunity to contemplate the beauty of our humanity, and the elevated potential that human beings may aspire to.

Such an ethos naturally expands outwards, seeking tranquility and justice on a global scale. Throughout Jewish history, Shabbat has served as a source of moral, spiritual, and psychological strength, providing a microcosm of a fairer, simpler, loftier, more beautiful and harmonious world that Jews throughout the ages have sought to create. In this sense, Shabbat is a preview of the messianic future.

Vast libraries have been dedicated to descriptions of this holy experience, and a myriad of comprehensive courses cover its laws, ideas, and importance. Yet, despite the scholarly attention that it has enjoyed, no external description can come close to describing the full all-encompassing experience of actually celebrating Shabbat. Throughout life, we intuit the existence of certain experiences that lie beyond the parameters of the adjectives and expressions that have thus far been invented to describe ordinary human experiences. Some elements of human existence simply defy linguistic encapsulation. Shabbat belongs firmly within this category. As with love, beauty, and meaning itself, it must be experienced.

When our ancestors stood at a blazing mountain in the Sinai desert and emphatically declared: "We will do and we will hear (*na'ase venishma*),"[1] they were not simply responding

---

1. Exodus 24:7.

to the gift of the Torah and Shabbat, nor were they making a statement limited to that particular place or time. Rather, they were outlining a way of life, an attitude towards the covenant that they were about to enter. The relationship between action and emotion is reciprocal, and acting to experience something can trigger previously unfelt emotions:

> Many people assume that the link between emotion and behavior is one-way: Emotions shape behavior. You love him, therefore you kiss him. You hate him, therefore you hit him. This view is incorrect. In fact, the relationship is reciprocal. Much of the time, behavior actually shapes emotion.[2]

While the Jewish people have been described as the People of the Book, Judaism is actually a way of existence that invites vigorous, immersive participation. No facet of the Jewish experience demonstrates this truth better that Shabbat.

Throughout these pages, I have reflected on one of the greatest creative acts in history – the creation of Shabbat. This work has analyzed some of the ripple effect that experiencing the splendor of Shabbat can have on our inner selves, on our souls, and on society around us, as well as the messianic and revolutionary significance of creating a day of rest, through which the creation of the universe was completed. And yet, as mentioned, words can only accompany us so far along the path to fulfillment.

---

2. Noam Shpancer, "Action Creates Emotion," *Psychology Today*, October 25, 2010.

Take one day in your week if you can or one moment on this day to transform these ideas into ideals. Disconnect. Breathe. Listen. Be present with family and friends. Tune in to others. Tune into yourself. Flatten the hierarchies. Recalibrate. Gain perspective. Reach out to others. Throw open the doors of your homes, synagogues, and hearts. Reach upwards towards the ultimate source of existence itself. Perhaps, in that magical moment when we light the Shabbat candles, we will silence the noise and hear, for just a brief moment, the music of our soul, and the eternal beat of our national heart.

Shabbat shalom!

About the Author

Rabbi Benji Levy is the CEO of Mosaic United, a joint venture partnership between Israel and global Jewry to strengthen Jewish identity and connections to Israel for youth around the world.

He served for six years as the Dean of Moriah College in Sydney, Australia, with over 1,800 pre-kindergarten through high school students. During this period he created a renaissance in Jewish life and was presented with the inaugural Australian Educator of the Year Award for his leadership and service to the community. Rabbi Benji was named by *Makor Rishon* as one of the top three 2019 change-makers working for world Jewry, is the author of the forthcoming *The New Old Path: Torah for the Twenty-First Century*, and frequently shares his thoughts through social media @Rabbi Benji. He holds a BA in Media and Communications and Honors in Jewish Civilization Thought & Culture from the University of Sydney and an Education degree from Herzog College in Israel. Following his study at Yeshivat Har Etzion he received rabbinic ordination and is currently completing his PhD in Jewish philosophy, for which he received the Australian Postgraduate Award.

Rabbi Benji lives in Jerusalem with his wife Renana and their children Shayna, Yehuda, Lital, and Amalia.

Maggid Books
The best of contemporary Jewish thought from
Koren Publishers Jerusalem Ltd.